EXOTIC FLOWERS
for Artists and Craftspeople

Yuko Green

DOVER PUBLICATIONS, INC.
Mineola, New York

Published in Canada by General Publishing Company, Ltd., 30 Lesmill Road, Don Mills, Toronto, Ontario.
Published in the United Kingdom by Constable and Company, Ltd., 3 The Lanchesters, 162–164 Fulham Palace Road, London W6 9ER.

Bibliographical Note

Exotic Flowers for Artists and Craftspeople is a new work, first published by Dover Publications, Inc., in 1997.

DOVER *Pictorial Archive* SERIES

Library of Congress Cataloging-in-Publication Data

Green, Yuko.
    Exotic flowers for artists and craftspeople / Yuko Green.
        p.   cm. — (Dover pictorial archive series)
    ISBN 0-486-29560-5 (pbk.)
    1. Flowers in art.   2. Decoration and ornament—Plant forms.   I. Title.   II. Series.
NK1560.G74   1997   96-45678
745.4—dc21   CIP

Manufactured in the United States of America
Dover Publications, Inc., 31 East 2nd Street, Mineola, N.Y. 11501

Publisher's Note

Yuko Green has chosen a variety of exotic flowers ranging from those popular as garden and house plants to more unusual tropical and wild flowers. The categories of flowering plants represented include trees, shrubs, ornamental herbs and vines spanning the five continents of North and South America, Asia, Africa and Australia and stretching through the South Pacific and Caribbean. (The category of plant and its native region are included in the captions.)

Demonstrating her aesthetic versatility, the artist presents rich and lush drawings that successfully combine recognizable naturalism with a touch of decorative stylization. The clarity of line will make reproduction, enlargement or reduction trouble-free, and of course all of the art (up to ten designs in any single project or publication) may be used without special permission.

Each flower is identified by its common (English) and scientific (Latin) names. When a flower is known by more than one common name (often there are even more), each of them used in the present book is provided in the captions and in the Alphabetical List of Common Names overleaf.

Alphabetical List of Common Names

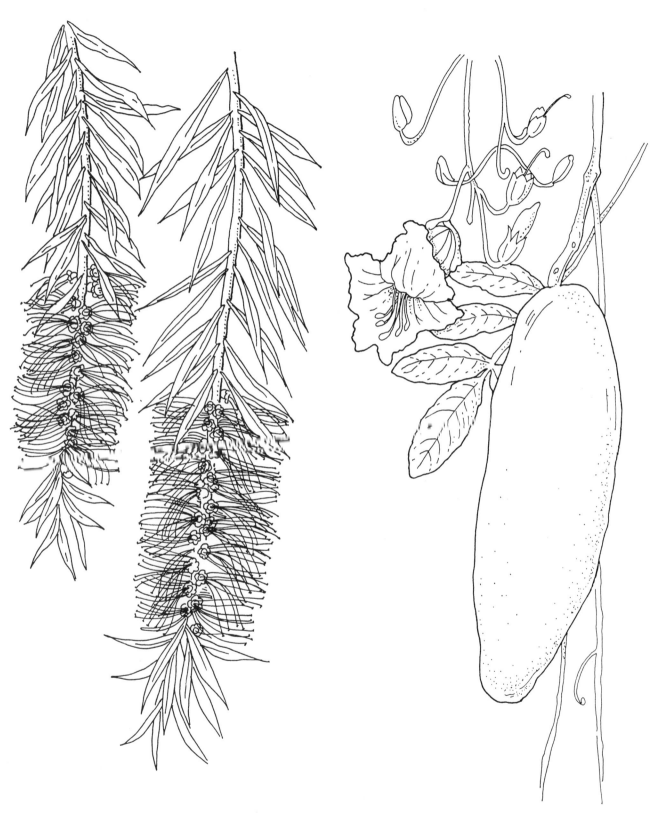

Bottlebrush Tree (*Callistemon lanceolatus*),
Australia (tree)

Sausage Tree (*Kigelia pinnata*),
tropical West Africa (tree)

1

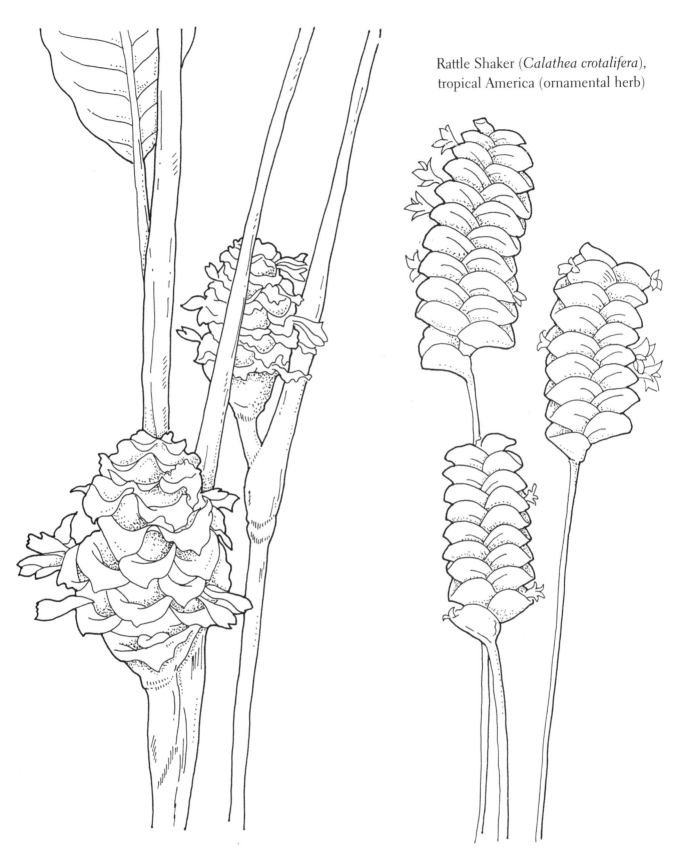

Rattle Shaker (*Calathea crotalifera*), tropical America (ornamental herb)

Calathea (*Calathea*), Brazil (ornamental herb)

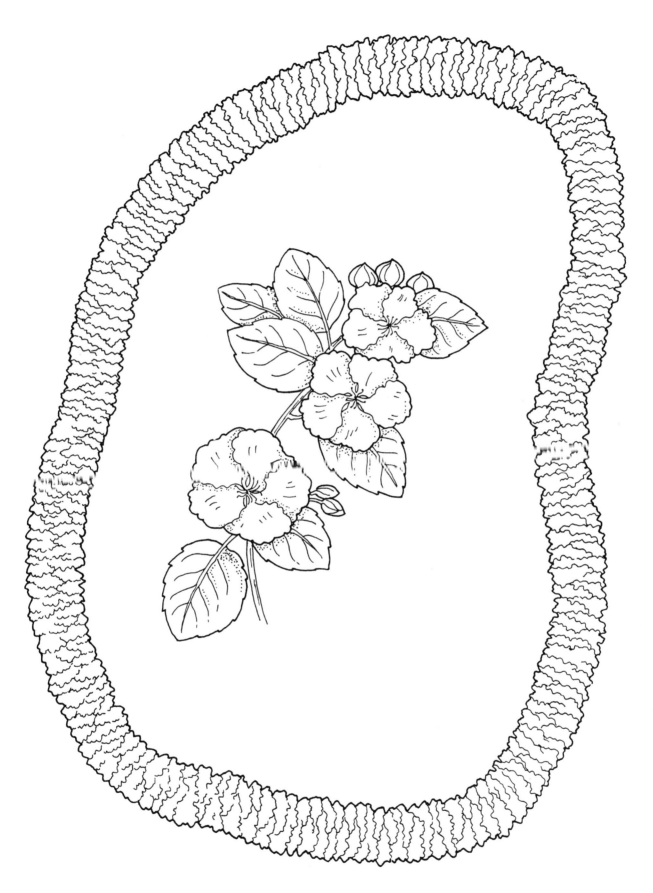

Ilima (*Sida fallax*), Hawaii and Pacific (shrub)

Stephanotis (*Stephanotis floribunda*), Madagascar (vine)

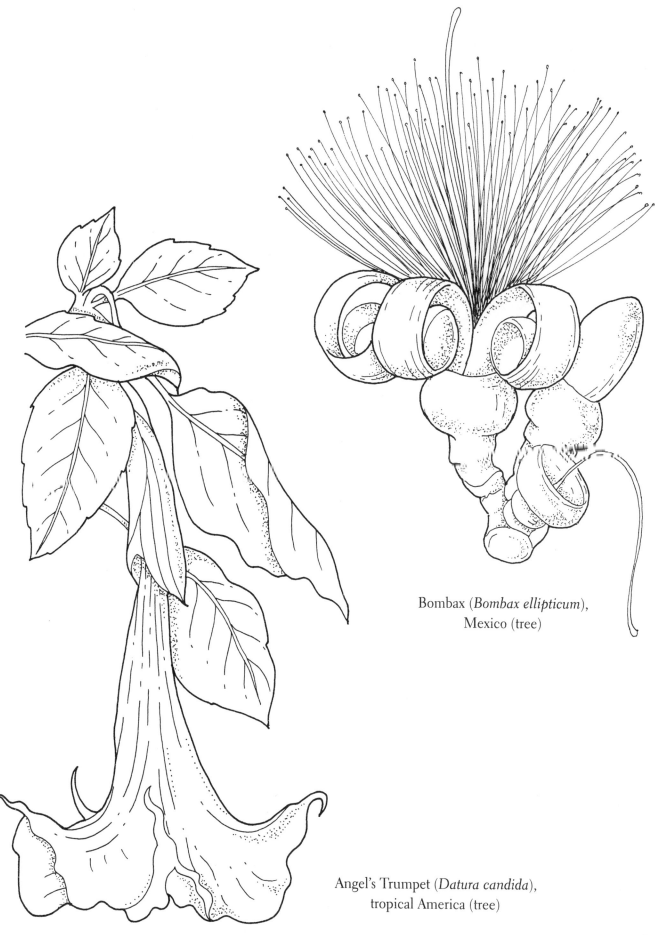

Bombax (*Bombax ellipticum*),
Mexico (tree)

Angel's Trumpet (*Datura candida*),
tropical America (tree)

Bifrenaria (*Bifrenaria*), Brazil (ornamental herb)

Lycaste (*Lycaste*), Venezuela, Colombia, Peru and Ecuador (ornamental herb)

Oleander (*Nerium oleander*),
Asia Minor and India (shrub)

Poinsettia (*Euphorbia pulcherrima*), Mexico (shrub)

Gold Tree (*Tabebuia donnell-smithii*),
Central America (tree)

Monkeypod / Rain Tree (*Samanea saman*), tropical America (tree)

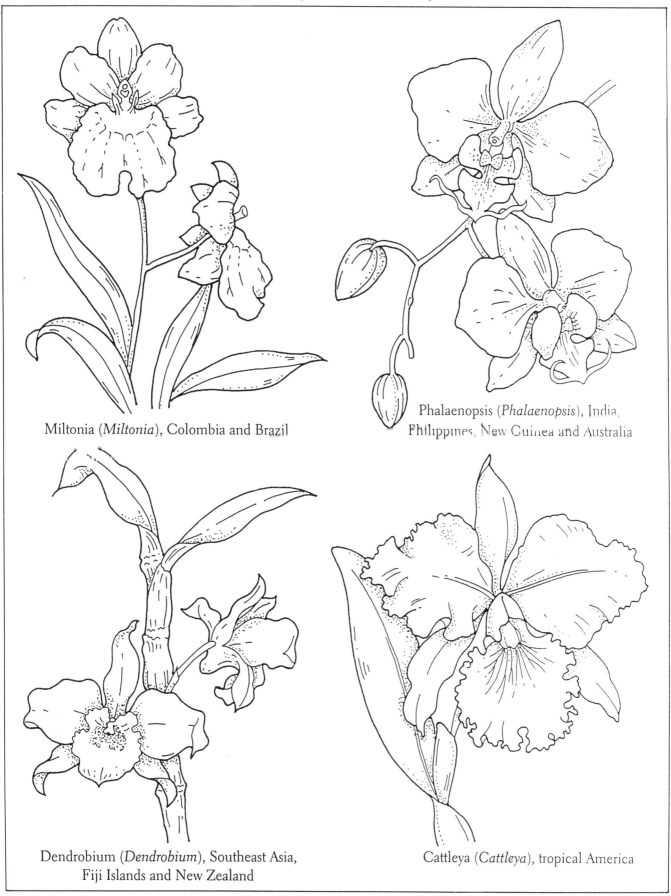

Miltonia (*Miltonia*), Colombia and Brazil

Phalaenopsis (*Phalaenopsis*), India,
Philippines, New Guinea and Australia

Dendrobium (*Dendrobium*), Southeast Asia,
Fiji Islands and New Zealand

Cattleya (*Cattleya*), tropical America

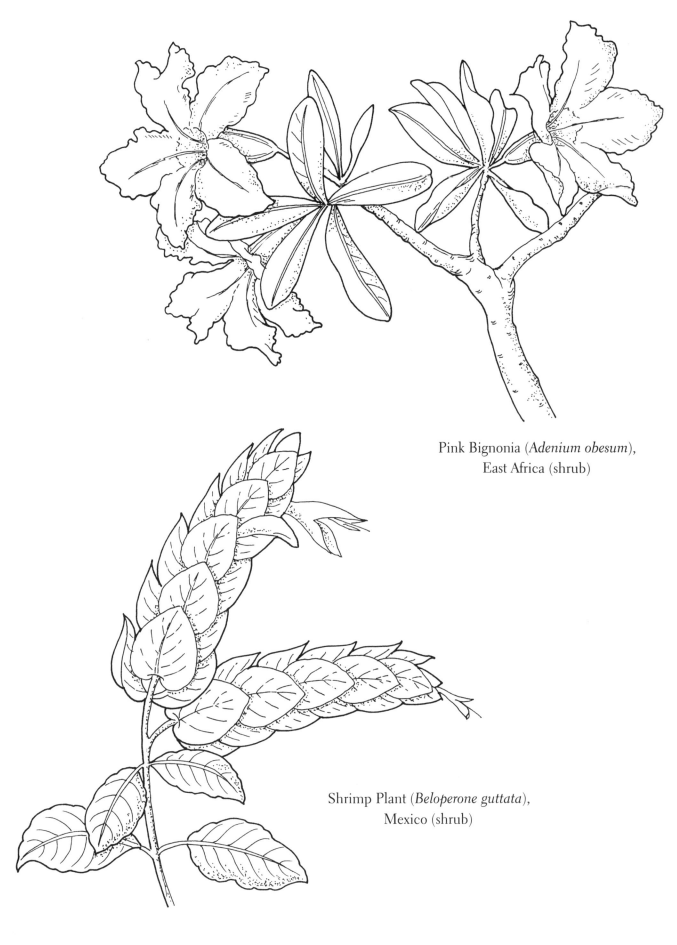

Pink Bignonia (*Adenium obesum*),
East Africa (shrub)

Shrimp Plant (*Beloperone guttata*),
Mexico (shrub)

Spathiphyllum (*Spathiphyllum*),
horticultural (ornamental herb)

Monstera (*Monstera*),
Central America (ornamental herb)

Indian Coral Tree / Tiger's Claw
(*Erythrina variegata*), tropical Asia (tree)

Be-still Tree (*Thevetia neriifolia*),
tropical America (tree)

Lei (Hawaiian garland) of white ginger

Crown Flower (*Calotropis gigantea*), India (shrub)

Rose Apple (*Eugenia jambos*),
India and Malaya (tree)

Umbrella Tree / Octopus Tree (*Brassaia actinophylla*), Australia (tree)

15

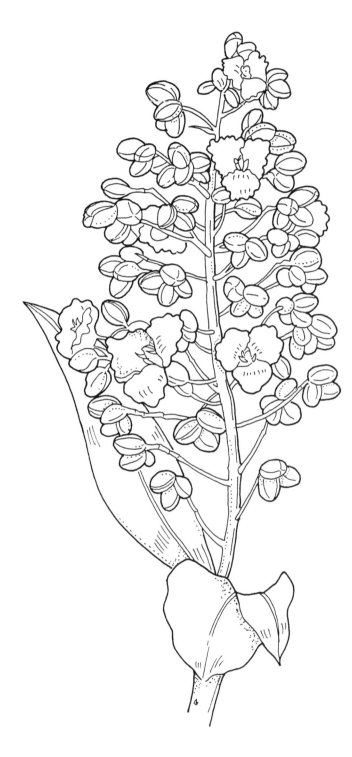

Blue Ginger (*Dichorisandra thyrsiflora*),
Brazil (ornamental herb)

Turmeric (*Curcuma domestica*),
India and Malaya (ornamental herb)

Chenille Plant (*Acalypha hispida*), India (shrub)

Ixora (*Ixora macrothyrsa*), East Indies (shrub)

Red Jade Vine (*Mucuna bennettii*),
New Guinea (vine)

Brazilian Glory (*Ipomoea horsfalliae*),
West Indies (vine)

18

St. Thomas Tree (*Bauhinia monandra*),
tropical America (tree)

Royal Poinciana (*Delonix regia*), Madagascar (tree)

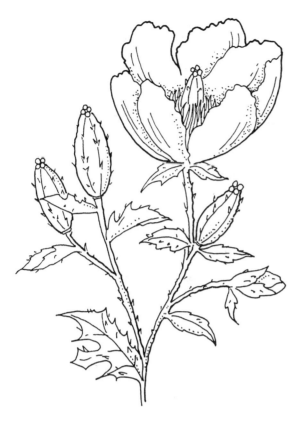

Prickly Poppy / Hawaiian Poppy (*Argemone glauca*),
Hawaii (ornamental herb)

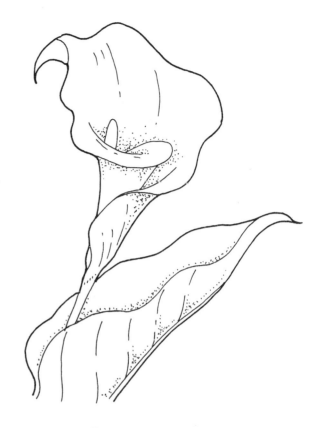

Calla Lily (*Zantedeschia*),
southern Africa (ornamental herb)

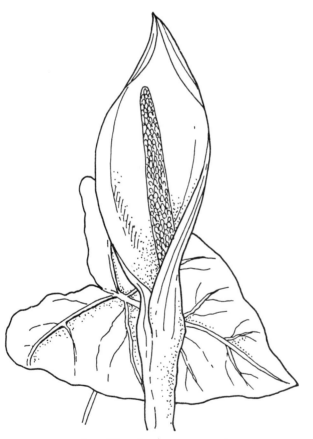

Ape (*Xanthosoma roseum*),
Central America (ornamental herb)

Canna (*Canna indica*),
tropical America (ornamental herb)

Candle Bush (*Cassia alata*),
tropical America (shrub)

Tecomaria (*Tecomaria capensis*),
South Africa (shrub)

21

Ohia-Lehua (*Metrosideros collinus*), Polynesia (tree)

Plumeria (*Plumeria acutifolia*), tropical America (tree)

A group of Bromeliads (Bromeliaceae), tropical America (ornamental herbs)

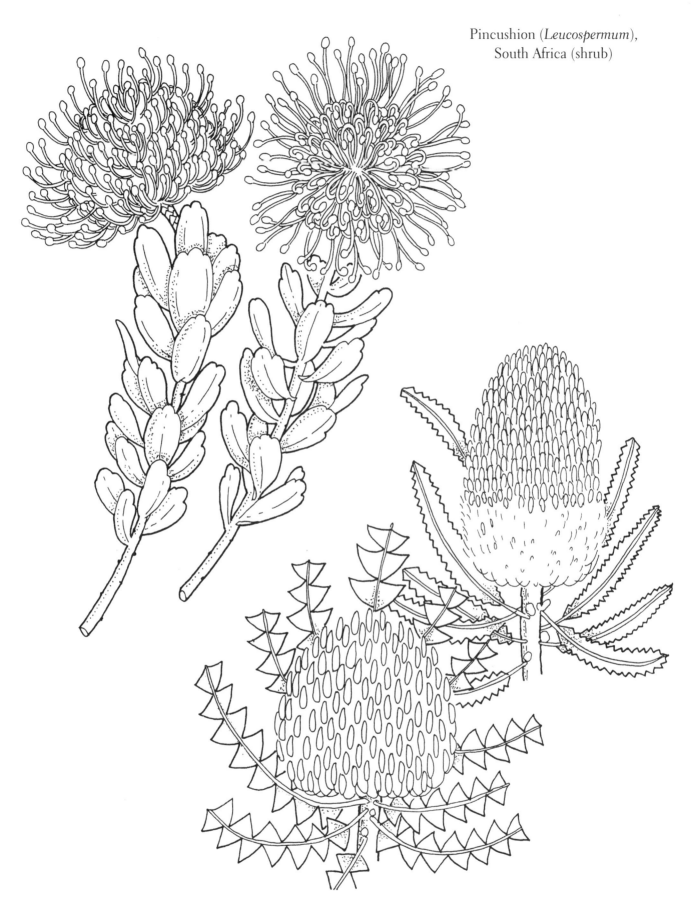

Pincushion (*Leucospermum*),
South Africa (shrub)

Two species of Banksia (*Banksia*), Australia (shrubs)

Yellow Allamanda (*Allamanda cathartica*), Brazil (vine)

Clematis (*Clematis paniculata*), Japan (vine)

Rainbow Shower Tree (*Cassia hybrida*
[*Cassia javanica* × *Cassia fistula*]), horticultural (tree)

Pink Tecoma Tree (*Tecoma pentaphylla*), tropical America (tree)

Spathiphyllum (*Spathiphyllum*),
horticultural (ornamental herb)

Anthurium / Flamingo Flower
(*Anthurium andraeanum*),
Colombia (ornamental herb)

Anthurium / Flamingo Flower (*Anthurium andraeanum*), Colombia (ornamental herb)

King Protea (*Protea cynaroides*), Africa (shrub)

Kou (*Cordia subcordata*), Polynesia (tree)

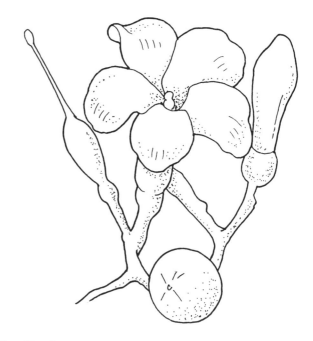

Pua-Kenikeni (*Fagraea berterana*), South Pacific (tree)

Tree Hibiscus / Hau (*Hibiscus tiliaceus*),
tropical cosmopolitan (tree)

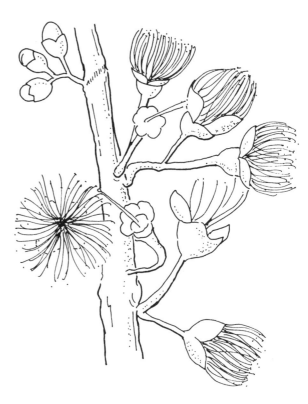

Mountain Apple (*Eugenia malaccensis*),
India and Malaya (tree)

A group of Gingers, East Indies and East Asia (ornamental herbs)

Hibiscus (*Hibiscus*), tropical cosmopolitan (shrubs)

Climbing Pandanus / Screwpine (*Freycinetia multiflora*),
Southeast Asia to Hawaii (vine)

'Ie'ie (*Freycinetia arborea*), Hawaii (vine)

Mangrove (*Bruguiera gymnorhiza*), Malaya and India to southern China (tree)

Brassavola (*Brassavola*),
tropical America (ornamental herb)

Tulip Orchid / Anguloa (*Anguloa*),
South America (ornamental herb)

Gardenia (*Gardenia jasminoides*), China (shrub)

Tahitian Gardenia / Tiare (*Gardenia taitensis*), Tahiti (shrub)

A lei of Plumeria (*Plumeria acutifolia*), tropical America (tree)

Spider Lily (*Pancratium littorale*),
tropical America (ornamental herb)

Indian Lotus (*Nelumbium nucifera*), India (ornamental herb)

Berzelia (*Berzelia galpinii*), South Africa (shrub)

Species of Protea (Proteaceae), Africa (shrubs)

Climbing Lily (*Gloriosa rothschildiana*),
tropical Africa (vine)

Large-flowered Thunbergia (*Thunbergia grandiflora*), India (vine)

Valencia Orange Tree (*Citrus sinensis*), Malaya and Indonesia (tree)

Lipstick Plant / Annatto (*Bixa orellana*), tropical America (shrub)

A group of Bromeliads (Bromeliaceae), tropical America (ornamental herbs)

Dwarf Poinciana (*Poinciana pulcherrima*),
tropical cosmopolitan (shrub)

Calliandra (*Calliandra inaequilatera*), Bolivia (shrub)

42

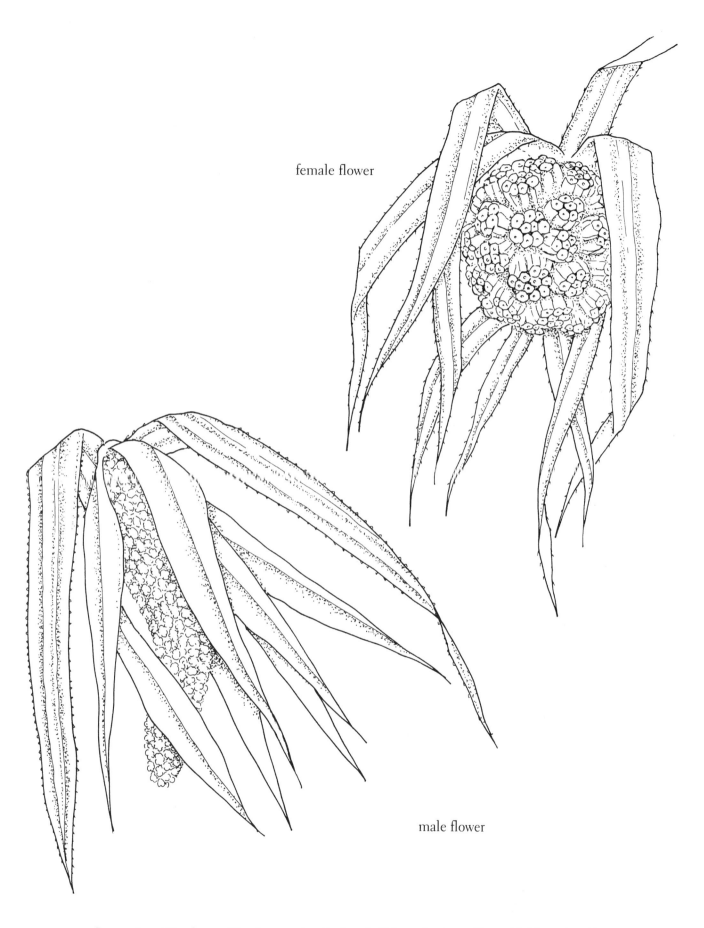

female flower

male flower

Screwpine / Pandanus (*Pandanus odoratissimus*), Polynesia, Australia and Malaya (tree)

A bouquet of Orchids (Orchidaceae), cosmopolitan (ornamental herbs) [and fern]

Species of Protea (Proteaceae), Africa (shrubs)

Canavalia / Mauna Loa Vine
(*Canavalia microcarpa*), Madagascar (vine)

Lei of canavalia

African Tulip (*Spathodea campanulata*), tropical Africa (tree)

Anthurium / Flamingo Flower (*Anthurium andraeanum*),
Colombia (ornamental herb)

Bird-of-Paradise (*Strelitzia reginae*),
South Africa (ornamental herb)

Poinsettia (*Euphorbia pulcherrima*), Mexico (shrub)

Plumeria (*Plumeria acutifolia*), tropical America (tree)

Orchid Tree (*Bauhinia variegata*), India (tree)

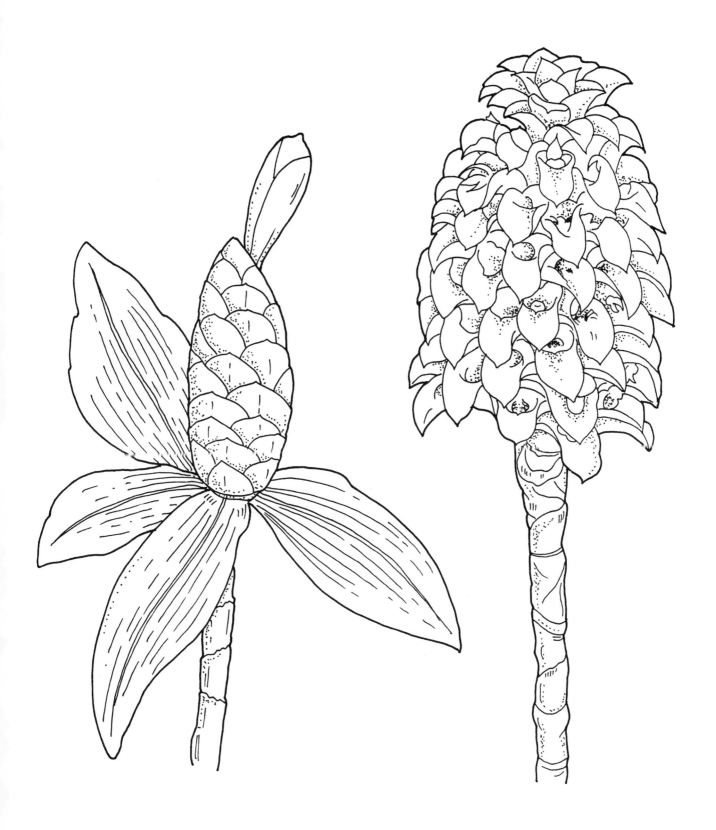

Orange Costus (*Costus scaber*),
Brazil (ornamental herb)

Indonesian Ginger (*Tapeinochilos ananassae*),
Indonesia (ornamental herb)

Beach Naupaka (*Scaevola frutescens*),
Hawaii (shrub)

Caper Bush (*Capparis cordifolia*),
Fiji and eastern Polynesia (shrub)

52

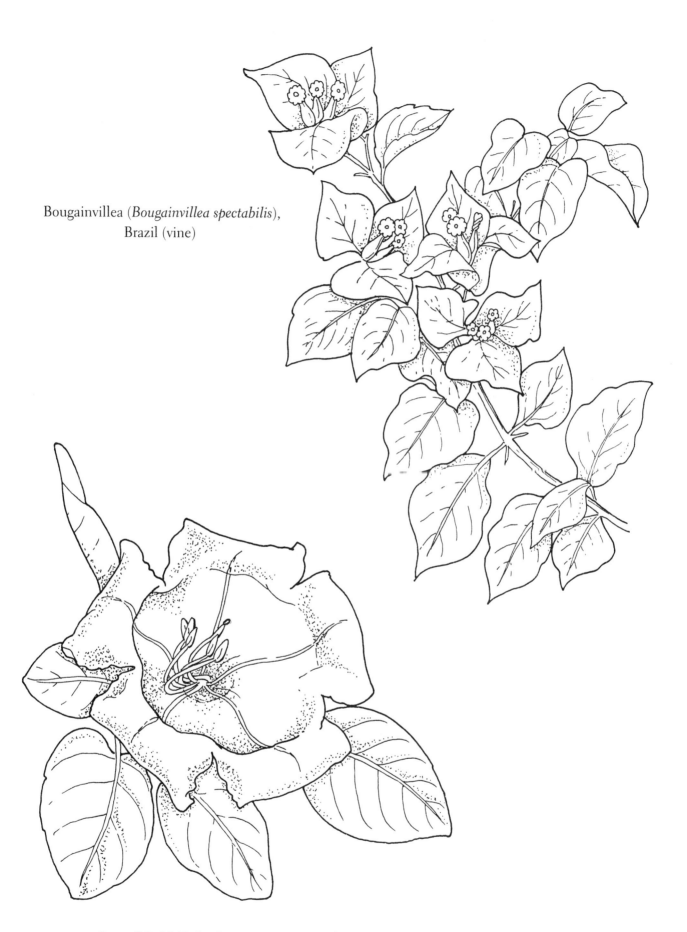

Bougainvillea (*Bougainvillea spectabilis*),
Brazil (vine)

Cup-of-Gold (*Solandra guttata*), Mexico (vine)

Autograph Tree (*Clusia rosea*), West Indies (tree)

A grouping of Heliconia (*Heliconia*), tropical America (ornamental herb)

Flametip (male flower) (*Leucodendron discolor*),
Africa (shrub)

Yellow Tulip (*Leucodendron laureolum*),
Africa (shrub)

Candlenut Tree (*Aleurites moluccana*),
Malaysia and Polynesia (tree)

Lei of candlenuts

Silversword (*Argyroxiphium sandwicense*), Hawaii (ornamental herb)

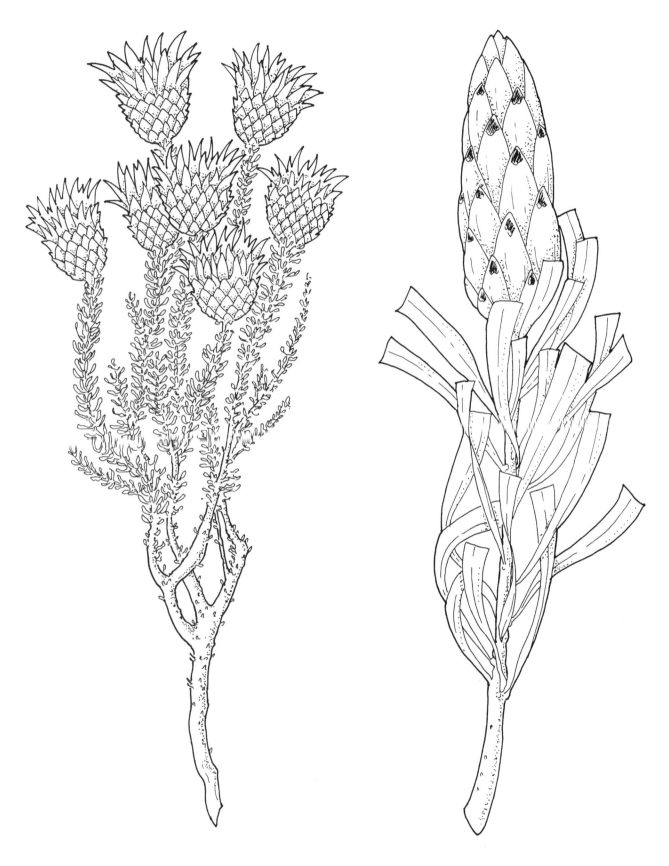

Phaenocoma (*Phaenocoma prolifera*),
South Africa (shrub)

Protea Repens (*Protea repens*),
Africa (shrub)

Wood Rose (*Ipomoea tuberosa*), tropical America (vine)

Orange Trumpet (*Phrostegia ignea*), Brazil (vine)

White Bird-of-Paradise (*Strelitzia nicolai*), South Africa (ornamental herb)

Safari Sunset (*Leucodendron* hybrid),
Australia and New Zealand horticultural (shrub)

Brunia (*Brunia albiflora*),
Africa (shrub)

Blushing Bride (*Serruria florida*),
South Africa (shrub)

Long-leaved Protea (*Protea longifolia*),
South Africa (shrub)

Heliconias (ornamental herbs)

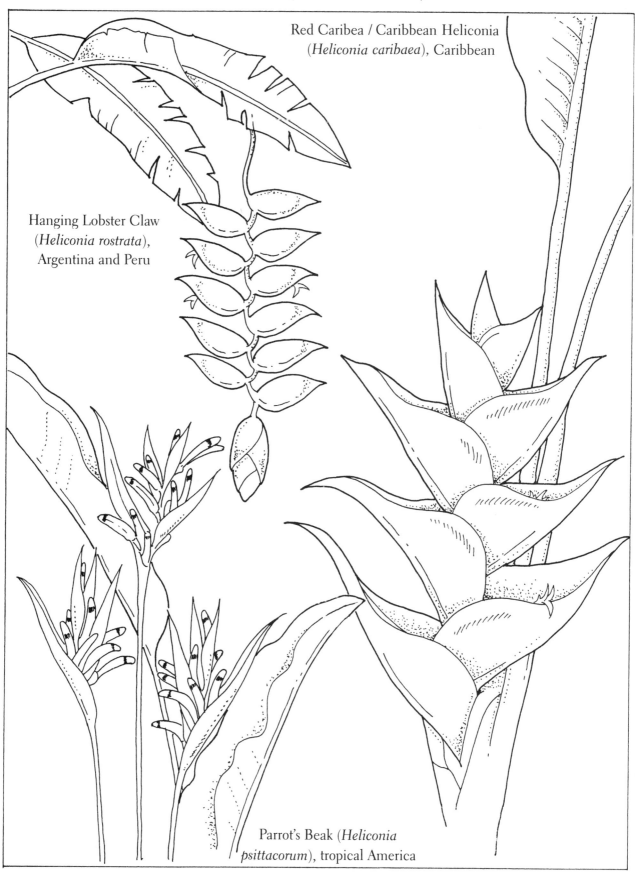

Red Caribea / Caribbean Heliconia
(*Heliconia caribaea*), Caribbean

Hanging Lobster Claw
(*Heliconia rostrata*),
Argentina and Peru

Parrot's Beak (*Heliconia psittacorum*), tropical America

Gingers (ornamental herbs)

Torch Ginger (*Phaeomeria magnifica*), Indonesia

Shell Ginger (*Alpinia nutans*), tropical East Asia

Red Ginger (*Alpinia purpurata*), East Indies

Crown of Thorns (*Euphorbia splendens*),
Madagascar (shrub)

Night-blooming Cereus (*Hylocereus*), Mexico (shrub)

Passion Flower (*Passiflora quadrangularis*), New World (vine)

Colvillea (*Colvillea racemosa*), Madagascar (tree)

Silk Oak (*Grevillea robusta*), Australia (tree)

Orchids (ornamental herbs)

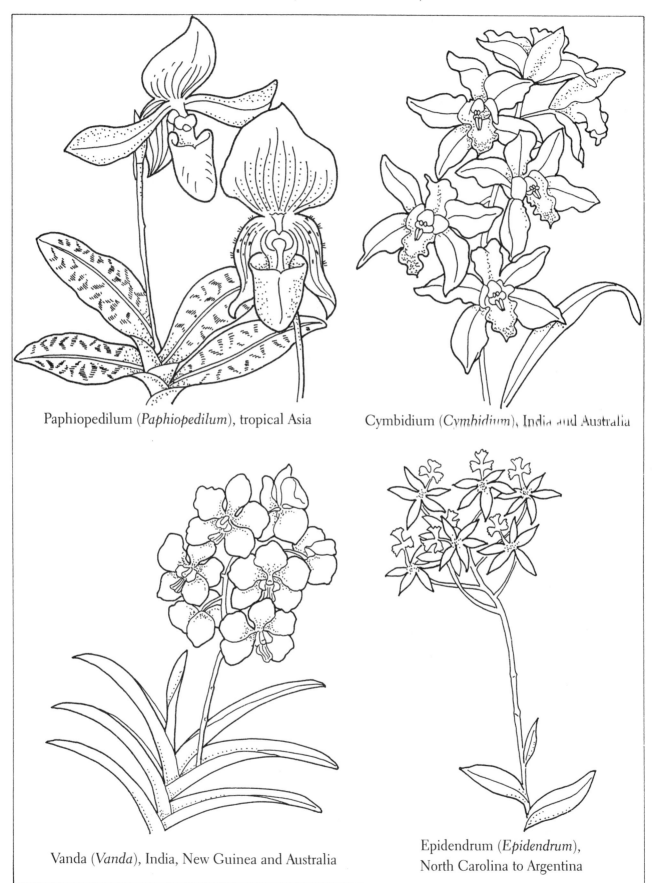

Paphiopedilum (*Paphiopedilum*), tropical Asia

Cymbidium (*Cymbidium*), India and Australia

Vanda (*Vanda*), India, New Guinea and Australia

Epidendrum (*Epidendrum*),
North Carolina to Argentina

Hibiscus (shrubs)

Butterfly Hibiscus (*Hibiscus*), horticultural

Hawaiian White Hibiscus
(*Hibiscus arnottianus*), Hawaii

Coral Hibiscus (*Hibiscus schizopetalus*), East Africa

Double Hibiscus (*Hibiscus*), horticultural

Chinese Red Hibiscus
(*Hibiscus rosa-sinensis*), South China

Gingers (ornamental herbs)

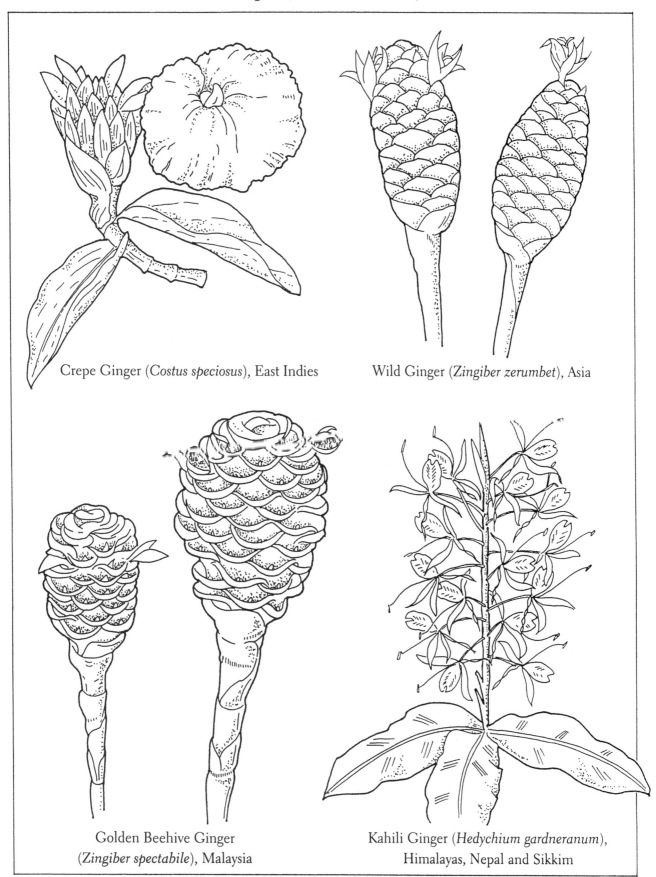

Crepe Ginger (*Costus speciosus*), East Indies

Wild Ginger (*Zingiber zerumbet*), Asia

Golden Beehive Ginger
(*Zingiber spectabile*), Malaysia

Kahili Ginger (*Hedychium gardneranum*),
Himalayas, Nepal and Sikkim

Lantana (*Lantana camara*),
tropical America (shrub)

Madagascar Periwinkle (*Vinca rosea*),
tropical America (shrub)

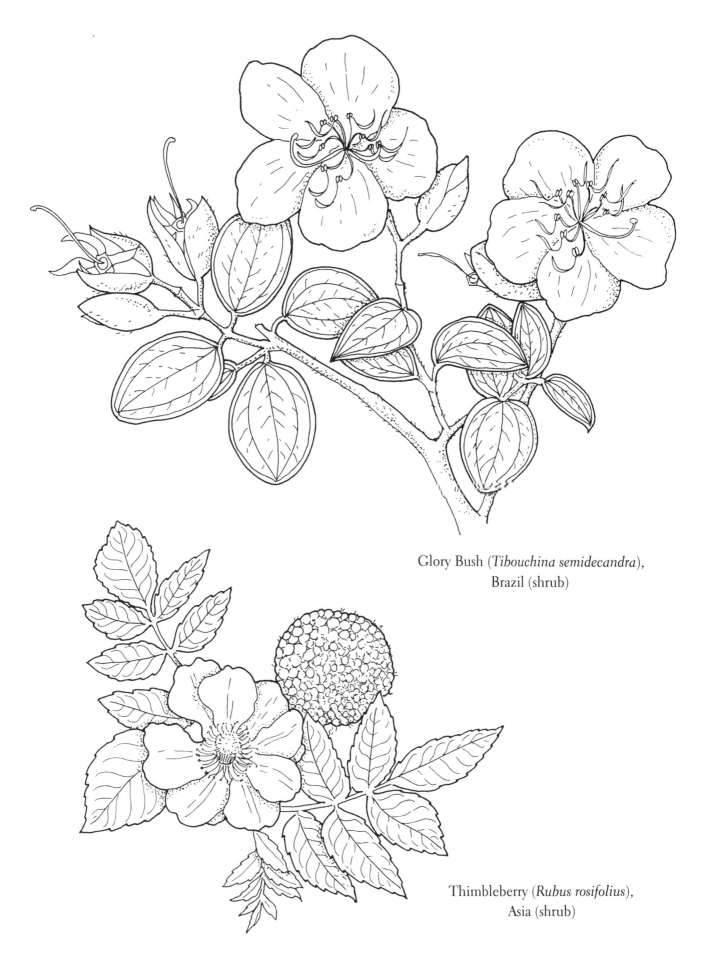

Glory Bush (*Tibouchina semidecandra*),
Brazil (shrub)

Thimbleberry (*Rubus rosifolius*),
Asia (shrub)

Pikake (*Jasminum sambac*), India (vine)